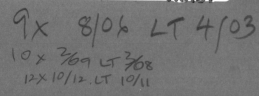

# CHINESE RAILROAD WORKERS

# CHINESE
# RAILROAD WORKERS
## SUSAN SINNOTT

*Franklin Watts*
*New York / Chicago / London /Toronto / Sydney*
*A First Book*

Cover photograph copyright ©: North Wind Picture Archives, Alfred, Me.

Photographs copyright ©: California State Library, California Section: pp. 8, 10, 12, 18; North Wind Picture Archives, Alfred, Me.: pp. 15, 20, 21, 27, 33, 41, 45, 47; California State Railroad Museum: pp. 23, 55; The Oakland Museum: p. 24; The Bettmann Archive: pp. 29, 30, 37; Collection of the New York Historical Society: p. 34; Collection of Gilcrease Museum, Tulsa, *Snow Sheds on the Central Pacific Railroad in the Sierra Nevada Mountains,* by Joseph Becker, oil, (#0136.1212): p. 43; Utah State Historical Society: p. 51; Anthony Barboza: p.58.

Library of Congress Cataloging-in-Publication Data

Sinnott, Susan
Chinese railroad workers / by Susan Sinnott
p.  cm. — (A First book)
Includes bibliographical references and index.
ISBN 0-531-20169-4
1. Railroad construction workers—West (U.S.)—History—19th century—Juvenile literature. 2. Chinese Americans—Employment— West (U. S.)—History — 19th century—Juvenile literature.  3. Central Pacific Railroad Company—History—Juvenile literature.
[1. Railroads—History. 2. Chinese Americans—History.] I. Title. II. Series.
HD8039.R3152U67   1994
331.7′61385′0951—dc20

94–50
CIP   AC

# CONTENTS

Chapter One
*Lost in the Clouds*
7

Chapter Two
*The Vision*
14

Chapter Three
*They Built the Great Wall of China, Didn't They?*
22

Chapter Four
*Cape Horn*
31

Chapter Five
*Summit Assault*
35

Chapter Six
*A Mile a Day in '68!*
42

Chapter Seven
*A Race to the Finish*
46

Chapter Eight
*Promontory and Beyond*
53

Chapter Nine
*Ghosts*
57

*For Further Reading*
61

*Index*
62

# 1

## LOST IN THE CLOUDS

At first the men worked knee deep in the snow, hacking at the hard, gray granite that would become the Summit Tunnel. Then they stood waist deep, still hammering at the immovable wall of stone. All the while the one-eyed, red-faced Yankee boss, James Strobridge, who never even pretended to like the Chinese workers in his charge, bellowed *Hurry! Hurry! Hurry!* Sometimes the white bosses came by with yardsticks. You moved the mountain only 1 foot (.3 m) in twenty-four hours, they would say. *Chinamen too slow! Too slow!*

Soon the men had to lay down their picks and spend all day just shoveling snow off the roadbed. Wherever they pitched it, gale force winds blew it back in their faces.

That first blizzard of the Sierra Nevada winter of 1866–67 was followed closely by another, then another. There were forty-four in all, according to

*Before the great snows: Chinese workers take a break from their work on the Summit Tunnel.*

those who could tell one from the other. Through December, at least, the Chinese crews kept punching through the infamous Summit Tunnel, high above Dutch Flat and just below Donner Pass. It was the highest, most exposed spot in the Sierras, and the snow never stopped falling.

In January 1867, construction chief Charles Crocker made the decision to cease work on the Summit until later in the spring. He moved three thousand Chinese workers to another unfinished tunnel farther down the mountain. Under snowdrifts of more than 40 feet (12 m), the men lived like moles, scurrying down narrow passageways from the tunnel worksite to their barracks and back again, never seeing the light of day. "We were in the tunnel so long," one worker remembered, "we learned to see many colors in black."

Back in San Francisco, no one was surprised when they heard about Charley Crocker's hard times in the High Sierras. They'd never believed the blustery Sacramento merchant could really take his Central Pacific Railroad over those rugged mountains anyway. It was too expensive and too difficult, they'd all said, and he'll never be able to hire enough able-bodied workers. But Charley Crocker had shown the doubters: He pulled together the money, the expertise, and seven thousand diligent

*Snowplows pushed by locomotive engines clear
the tracks so supply trains can reach the crews.*

Chinese. He'd just forgotten to convince Mother Nature to be on his side.

In late February 1867, the season's worst blizzard brought a blinding curtain of snow. Strong winds blew—"raging and howling like a madman," according to one observer—for five straight days, moving snow cleared from the completed tracks into 60-foot (18-m) drifts. When the winds finally subsided, the snows began to fall again, accumulating on cuts, trails, and camps. Locomotives were fixed behind snowplows to push through the huge drifts and pull along the all-important supply trains. When the engines slowed to a halt, thousands of Chinese emerged from their tunnels to dig them out.

As the snows piled higher on the upper mountain ridges, the danger of avalanches increased as well. Earlier attempts to hack away at the giant snowbanks high above the Donner Pass had proven futile. When workers heard the unmistakable distant roar, they simply waited, helpless, for the crush of snow, dirt, and rocks. Frozen bodies, often still clutching shovels and picks, were recovered the next spring, if ever. No one really knew how many Chinese were carried away in these avalanches; sometimes one or two were missing when worked resumed, sometimes whole teams were gone.

*Charles Crocker supervises the construction of snow sheds that will allow the Chinese to work through even the harshest snows.*

Late that spring twelve thousand men returned to the Summit Tunnel to pick through the thick snow and ice of their abandoned sites. Even under the sparkling blue Sierra skies, the going was very tough. Crocker and Strobridge had ordered an all-out attack on a 40-mile (64-km) stretch from the summit (above the Donner Pass) to the Sierra range's eastern base. The Chinese, as usual, did the work of twice their number. But, in October 1867, with the infamous Summit Tunnel far from finished and a 7-mile (11.2-km) gap in the rail line still open like a gaping wound, the snows came once again. This winter, so the locals said, would likely be just as bad as the last one.

In November 1867, a few reporters visited the base quarters to hear firsthand about the railroad's progress. The news was dismal. The newspapermen returned to their cities and quickly spread the word around the nation that, just as everyone had expected, Charley Crocker and his Chinese army were indeed "lost in the clouds of the Sierra."

# 2

## THE VISION

The early story of the building of America's transcontinental railroad is one of men who, during their lifetimes, were thought crazy or foolish or both. During the beginning of the nineteenth century, a few politicians and journalists wrote articles and gave fiery speeches telling how the rail line would finally link Europe to Asia, thereby completing the work of Columbus. For their trouble, they were taken to task by the likes of Daniel Webster, who stood before Congress and asked, "What would we do with the Western coastline, 3,000 miles [4,800 km] away, rockbound, cheerless and uninviting?"

By the 1850s, however, many forward-thinking Americans realized the time had come for rail service across the continent. Clearly, traveling overland by stagecoach or wagon train was both slow and dangerous. To sail coast to coast meant a 5,426-mile (8,730-km), thirty-day journey via the Isthmus

*Before the railroad was complete, transcontinental travelers needed to cross the Isthmus of Panama.*

of Panama. (A passenger heading west would sail to the eastern coast of Panama, then, after a 51-mile [81.6-km] overland trek, board another ship to complete the journey north to California. The Panama Canal wasn't built until 1914.) The alternative was a tiresome six-month journey around the tip of South America's Cape Horn.

When Congress and the president finally agreed that a railroad should be built, the question became where? Across which states or territories? Should the terminus be Seattle, San Francisco, or Los Angeles? Smelling profits and power, many politicians rejected government survey maps and insisted their cities or states should become the new railroad centers. So, with no agreement on which, if any, of the government surveys to use, the whole undertaking became hopelessly deadlocked.

Reports of the stalled project were read with great interest by a smart young surveyor from Massachusetts named Theodore Dehone Judah. Judah was not only a dedicated railroader, he was an unstoppable optimist. He knew a transcontinental railroad could be built, and he also knew he was the one to do it. He was crazy, yes, fanatical, maybe—a visionary, definitely.

Judah had looked over the government's survey maps and spotted several problems. One, he told anyone in Washington who would listen, was that, for geological and topographical reasons, the terminus had to be San Francisco, not Seattle or Los Angeles. Next, the only reasonable route over the forbidding Sierra Mountains was via the Donner Pass, not around Lake Tahoe, as everyone had always insisted.

To prove his point, Judah walked the rocky trails and climbed the mountains, pinpointing every relevant detail until he was absolutely certain of his railroad's route. Then, with startling boldness and confidence, he set out to start up a railroad company that would make use of his own maps. He spoke before countless potential investors, winning the nickname "Crazy Judah" for his ability to talk for hours about his railroad.

After many fruitless meetings in San Francisco, Judah headed for Sacramento, where he envisioned construction would begin. His first discussions were not encouraging. Finally, at a gathering of a dozen Sacramento businessmen above a downtown hardware store, Judah detected a spark of real interest. This railroad will link Sacramento with Nevada's silver mines, he told those assembled, and the markets beyond. Those who get in on the ground floor will become rich, he added, maybe the richest men in California. His audience quickly came to life. By the evening's end, four of the men had signed on: Collis P. Huntington and Mark Hopkins, who owned the hardware store one floor below, Leland Stanford, a politically ambitious grocer, and Charles Crocker, a dry goods merchant. To prove their interest, each gave Mr. Judah's Central Pacific Railroad $35,000 on the spot.

Collis P. Huntington

Mark Hopkins

Leland Stanford

Charles Crocker

On June 28, 1861, the Central Pacific Railroad Company was incorporated, with the four businessmen as officers. Theodore Judah, who had no business experience, was named chief engineer.

Before long, however, Theodore Judah became frustrated with his four associates, who seemed only interested in fat government construction subsidies. For their part, the four Californians had no confidence in this wild-eyed dreamer and began looking for ways to force Judah out of the company. After one stormy San Francisco meeting of the Central Pacific board, Judah did walk out, vowing to replace these know-nothings with East Coast investors who would help him take his company back. He sailed immediately to New York.

In fact, many wealthy Easterners were suddenly interested in the transcontinental railroad. They, just like their California counterparts, were becoming aware of its full money-making potential. Why now? On June 20, 1862, President Abraham Lincoln had signed into law the Pacific Railroad Act. This act spelled out the specifics for the building of the railroad, including how much money the U.S. government would loan for construction. The subsidy would be $16,000 per mile on flat land, $48,000 per mile in the Rocky and Sierra Nevada mountains, and $32,000 per mile for land in between the two

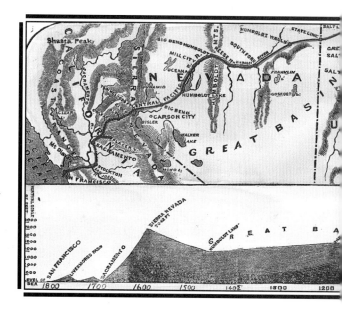

*Map and profile map of the Central Pacific Railroad from Omaha, Nebraska, to San Francisco, California*

mountain ranges. The Act also stated that the independent Central Pacific would build from California east and the government-managed Union Pacific would begin in Omaha, Nebraska, and head west. The two roads would connect at a place to be determined at a future date "not later than July 1, 1867."

Late that summer, Theodore Judah arrived back in California with a copy of the act, ready to patch up relations with his partners. He quickly discovered, however, that the rift between them had become a chasm. Already the four were scheming to find ways to gain even greater subsidies than the government allowed. Deeply discouraged, Judah

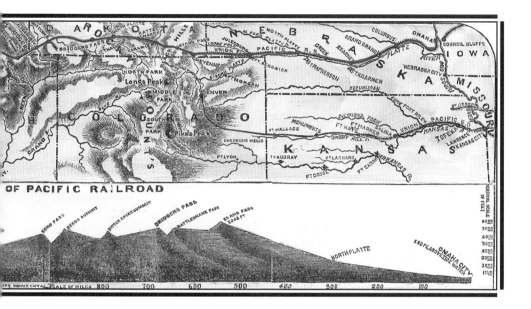

accepted their buyout offer of $100,000 for his part of the Central Pacific and set sail for New York. Once there, he intended to pay a visit to Commodore Vanderbilt, one of America's richest men, and propose a takeover of the Central Pacific.

But, the Central Pacific Railroad would never be his again.

In October 1862, Theodore Judah caught yellow fever during his journey across the Isthmus of Panama. He died shortly after arriving in New York. Central Pacific's Big Four, who were now truly free of interference from any crazy idealist, sent condolences to Judah's widow, Anna, and went about the business of building a Pacific railroad.

# 3 THEY BUILT THE GREAT WALL OF CHINA, DIDN'T THEY?

Everything moved more slowly than anyone—certainly the Central Pacific's money men—would have wanted. There were problems, to be sure, and some not so little. The Civil War demanded the full attention of President Lincoln and the Congress. Many New York bankers, so badly needed by both the Central Pacific (CP) and the Union Pacific (UP), had decided military hardware was a better investment than some wild-eyed scheme thousands of miles in the hinterlands.

Ground-breaking finally took place in Sacramento in January 1863. By 1865, however, only 31 miles (49.6 km) of track was complete and the company was virtually out of money. CP president, and now also the governor of California, Leland Stanford was doing everything possible to find money so construction could continue.

Central Pacific's only consolation was that their rival, the Union Pacific, was having an even harder

*Railroad construction supply docks in
Sacramento, California*

time. Six months after breaking ground in Omaha,
Nebraska, the UP's construction team was still
inside the city limits.

Meanwhile, out on the CP's railbed, construction problems of a different kind were looming.
Charles Crocker, the tough-talking construction
chief, had advertised throughout the West for five

thousand able-bodied workers. But the Civil War and the Nevada silver mines had lured many men away, and Charley Crocker was dismayed when no more than eight hundred came forward. Desperate, Crocker considered bringing in men from famine-stricken Ireland. Irishmen, after all, had already proven themselves good railroaders for the Union Pacific. The cost of bringing thousands of men from Europe around the tip of South America was, however, prohibitive.

*Many workers from Ireland helped build the Union Pacific Railroad.*

Finally Crocker asked, What about the Chinese? Weren't there thousands of them on the West Coast already, working for next to nothing in restaurants and laundries? Besides, aren't they very good with explosives? Strong resistance came from foreman James Strobridge, a sour-spirited Yankee. "I will not boss Chinese," he said. ". . . they're not fit laborers anyway."

The average Chinaman, as he pointed out, didn't weigh more than 110 pounds (50 kg). How could we, he told Crocker, take this railroad up over the High Sierras with only the efforts of these rice-eating weaklings? But Crocker, who was not usually so independent minded, came back with, "Hadn't the ancestors of these 'weaklings' built the Great Wall of China?"

Strobridge, who did not flinch at being called "racist," finally agreed to hire fifty Chinese and bring them to the CP's base quarters. The Celestials, as Strobridge called them, attracted menacing stares when they stepped off the hauler that had brought them to Dutch Flat from Sacramento. The Yankee and Irish crews had never seen men in dishpanlike straw hats and baggy blue pajamalike clothes, which were the typical Chinese dress of the time. They scoffed, too, at their long hair, which was worn in a single pigtail, or queue. Rumor had it that they also took baths every day and rinsed with flower water. Surely no dainty Chinaman could do a job meant for a strong Yank!

The Chinese ignored the hoots and hisses and set about making their camp. They were, after all, used to the hostile reactions of most white Americans. They awoke early the next morning and took up their picks, shovels, and wheelbarrows, and began their long work day. At the end of twelve hours, Crocker and Strobridge inspected the results. They were awestruck. Not only had the Chinese workers not fallen over from exhaustion, as many had expected, they had done the work of twice their number.

Crocker immediately hired fifty more, then another fifty. Before long, the Central Pacific was looking for any healthy Chinese male who wanted steady work and $30 a month salary. Within six months, two thousand Chinese were bringing the railroad ever closer to the Sierras.

From then on, work on the line progressed beyond the hopes of the Big Four. When the West Coast Chinatowns were emptied of able-bodied men, Crocker sought out a labor contractor who brought farm workers from China's Kwangtung (Guangdong) province. Many came from the area known as Sze Yup, the home of China's greatest seamen and adventurers. They accepted passage money loaned by agents—$40 to travel by steamship and $25 to $35 by sailing vessel—which they had to repay at high rates of interest once they began working.

After arriving on a crowded ship in San Francisco, the Chinese were met by CP employees

*Chinese emigrating to the United States had to endure long voyages on overcrowded steamships.*

and sent to Sacramento. There, they were divided into small teams of twelve to twenty men, each with their own foreman and cook. The head was a Chinese who'd been in California long enough to understand both the English language and the American way of business. He served as interpreter and clerk, collecting the workers' wages and deducting money for the labor agency.

The foreman also made sure fresh food was brought in regularly from Chinatown. The labor agreements stated that each Chinese crew or team would have their own cook, who would prepare dishes in the Cantonese tradition. There were dried oysters, fish, abalone, dried fruits, dried mushrooms, bamboo shoots, noodles, salted cabbage, peanut-oil crackers and candies, and an astonishing variety of meat, poultry, pork, and vegetables.

Of course, there were also rice and tea. The Chinese workers refused plain water, which was routinely served on the track to the Irish workers. Instead, Chinese tea prepared in barrels was carried up and down the track by the cooks' assistants. It was poured into tiny porcelain cups just like those "as ladies see fit to use," according to the disapproving Irish workers.

Despite such seemingly unusual requests, Charley Crocker favored the Chinese workers so much that they became known sarcastically as

*A Chinese tea carrier in front of the east end of
Tunnel #8 in the Sierra Nevada Mountains, 1867*

"Charley's pets." And, in truth, they were a bonanza for him. Even though he paid them the same monthly salary as the whites, he deducted the cost of room and board from their wages and made them work longer days. By hiring—and exploiting—the Chinese, he was able to lower his labor costs by one-third.

Most newspapers didn't write kindly about either the Chinese or Charles Crocker. As more and more Chinese signed on for railroad work, the

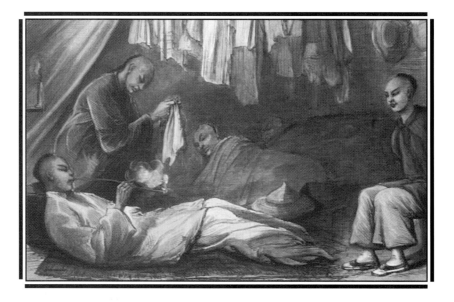

*Chinese workers settle into their tent for the night.*
*Images such as this one helped perpetuate the notion that*
*many Chinese were addicted to opium.*

California press began to talk openly about the
Yellow Peril. *The Chinese are taking jobs from the
whites!* the headlines exclaimed.

Charley Crocker, however, was as thick-skinned
as they come, and remained unperturbed by the
public and private criticism. By the end of 1865, he
had seven thousand Chinese in his employ—by the
end of 1866 the number would be twelve thousand—and was ready to take on the mountains of
the Sierra Nevada.

# 4
## CAPE HORN

Early in 1866, James Strobridge stared up at Cape Horn, the rocky spur that stood 2,000 feet (600 m) above the gorge of the American River, 57 miles (91.2 km) east of Sacramento. It was a shale mass, seemingly impenetrable. He looked down at the official Judah survey, which indicated the rail line would run along a ledge 1,400 feet (427 m) above the river.

Strobridge shook his head and thought to himself, I can describe how the job should be done, but where will I find a crew with nerve enough to do it?

The Chinese people, as Strobridge soon learned, had been carving roadways out of the sides of cliffs for thousands of years. This ancient art of engineering is even depicted in a famous painting from A.D. 775 that shows the mountaintop retreat of Emperor Hsuan-tsung. On a sheer face of rock, one can see a winding road that leads to the perch. The road seems to have been not so much built on the rock as *placed* there by a supernatural power. Strobridge would draw on these same engineering skills to fix his railroad tracks along this rocky ledge.

The Chinese railworkers wasted no time proving they, too, could carve a roadbed from a wall of rock. First, they wove baskets of tall reeds and vines. These baskets, large enough to hold two or three workers along with their sledges, iron hand drills, and a keg of black powder, were inscribed with Chinese characters asking for special good luck. Ropes were tied to side eyelets, and the baskets were slowly lowered from the cliff's edge down to the site of the future railroad bed, hundreds of feet below.

With the wind gusting and the baskets scraping against the mountains, the workers bored tiny holes into the face of Cape Horn, tamped the holes full of blasting powder, and set the fuses. Then, at a given signal, the baskets were raised just high enough to put the men out of harm's way. The rock broke into small bits and sprayed a wide area with shrapnel.

Slowly, daily, weekly, they moved the railbed around fearsome Cape Horn. And, when the task was completed in May 1866, even James Strobridge was heard to say, I think they can do anything.

To be sure, there were times when "anything" would be put to the test. The crew reached Dutch

*Chinese workers were lowered over the cliff's edge in handwoven baskets to set the powder fuses that would blast the rock and help turn this sheer cliff face into a rail line.*

*Passengers enjoy one of the first rides around the completed track on the infamous Cape Horn, 1866.*

Flat, California, in July 1866 and by November train service was open between Sacramento and Cisco, a distance of 94 miles (150.4 km). By the end of 1866, Charles Crocker spoke with pride of the 28 miles (44.8 km) of track completed that year by his workers. He spoke less often, in public anyway, about the tough challenges still ahead.

# 5

## SUMMIT ASSAULT

Cisco, a small logging town, became the base of operation for the Central Pacific's all-out assault on the High Sierras. From this point, the grade became much rougher and the difficult work of building fifteen tunnels and many trestles would start. Cisco itself was 6,000 feet (1,829 m) above sea level, but the highest location on the survey map was still 1,100 very steep feet (335.3 m) above. The 14-mile (22.4-km) route to the summit was cut by gorges and tree-covered ridges.

The important tunnel work, which had begun the year before, was proceeding slowly when the snows began to fly early that fall of 1866. More cautious men than Charles Crocker would have taken those October blizzards as a signal to quit for the winter. Charley decided, however, that a full-scale assault on the feared Tunnel No. 6 was the more appropriate course of action.

The Summit Tunnel, which was 38 miles (60.8 km) above Dutch Flat, 124 feet (37.8 m) below the summit of the infamous Donner Pass, and 7,032 feet (2,143.3 m) above sea level, would be the highest of the fifteen Sierra tunnels. More fearsome even than the height, however, was the hardness of the rock. The upper ridges of the summit were made of granite so solid the heaviest blasts of gunpowder left it unpenetrated. Nor did the granite give way to continuous blows of picks and chisels. Instead, the tools were left flattened and useless.

To break through the stubborn granite, the Central Pacific engineers decided to try out a new liquid explosive called nitroglycerin. As effective as nitroglycerin was—five times more powerful than powder explosives—its chemical instability made it very dangerous. Any jerky movement and the heated liquid would simply explode in the hands of an unsuspecting worker. The lives of many Chinese were lost because of this unpredictable mixture.

Early in 1866 James Strobridge himself lost an eye while standing too close to an accidental blast. From then on, the Chinese referred to him as the "one-eye bossy man" and, with his black patch, he became more intimidating than ever.

With Strobridge's accident, however, CP officials finally decided to return to the safer, more reli-

*A steam engine uses newly finished track to bring supplies to crews in the Sierra Nevadas.*

able—but less effective—blasting powder. (In 1866 Alfred Nobel, who invented nitroglycerin, perfected dynamite, which is a powerful but stable explosive. Several CP engineers knew about dynamite, but it was never tested or used by the company.)

Throughout the summer and fall of 1866, work on the Summit Tunnel proceeded from both its west and east ends and from above, where a shaft was chipped outward from the middle. The Chinese worked shoulder to shoulder in twelve-hour shifts, pecking, chipping, and hacking at the hard rock face. Despite this massive human effort, they advanced at 1 foot (.3 m) every twenty-four hours.

The white bosses, the "demons," as the Chinese called them, urged them to work harder and faster. Under the appalling conditions of the winter of 1866–67, the Chinese pushed and pushed. As they watched their fellow countrymen buried by snowslides, resentment over their unequal working conditions began to simmer. Finally, when that winter's bitter cold was just a memory, Chinese anger boiled over.

No one ever expected the patient, diligent Chinese to strike, but on June 24, 1867, three thousand tunnelmen, graders, and road clearers laid down their tools—picks, shovels, drills, and axes—and stopped working. They demanded a raise in pay from $30 to $45 per month and an end to their twelve-hour work day. "Eight hours a day good for white man, all the same good for Chinaman," they repeated over and over.

The Chinese sat quietly along the track while their spokesmen negotiated with the bosses. Not surprisingly, perhaps, Crocker and Strobridge showed no sympathy for *their* workers. Charles Crocker harangued the Chinese spokesmen and screamed that he would never give in to such demands. But the Chinese were ready to wait it out, knowing full well Crocker needed them badly: "No China Men, no railroad," they repeated.

Crocker, for his part, knew how to make life difficult for his "pets." He cut off their provisions—no dried abalone, no sweet and sour pork from Chinatown butchers, no food at all—and saw that they were confined to their camps. Finally, the Chinese gave in. They did receive a monthly pay hike of $5, but the twelve-hour day remained in place. The Chinese, who felt alone and vulnerable in this foreign world and who also had many dependent relatives back home in China, decided not to press their case further.

As the next harsh winter bore down with all its fury and work on the summit was forced to stop once again, disturbing news came from CP partner Collis Huntington in New York City. Word was spreading that Charley Crocker and his Central Pacific crews were hopelessly trapped in the Sierras; investors in New York and San Francisco were becoming nervous. Rumor had it, too, that the Union Pacific, which had moved swiftly across the Great Plains, was aiming to head into California and meet the CP on their home turf. This would, of course, be an outrage to Charles Crocker and the Californians of the Central Pacific.

Charley Crocker, however, was never one to sit back and wait for bad news to overwhelm him. If the money men wanted proof of progress, he declared, they shall have it. Just before the end of 1867, he gathered together every grader idled by the heavy snows, had them load sixteen thousand rails—each weighing 600 pounds (272.4 kg)—onto ox-driven snow sledges. He then asked—no, *ordered*—the Chinese to drag, push, and slide the cargo across the Sierras as soon as possible.

Then Crocker had forty rail cars attached to locomotives, filled those with tools and supplies, and sent them along the snow-covered tracks. Where the track was incomplete or simply disappeared into snow drifts, the locomotives were rolled on logs across treacherous ground. At Donner Lake, everything was moved once again to reinforced wagons for the trip to the Truckee River. The caravan made dangerous detours around unfinished tunnels and bridges but it, too, went over the Sierras, down the eastern slope, and crossed the Nevada line.

This daring feat, which one reporter compared to Hannibal's crossing of the Alps with elephants, allowed the Central Pacific to reach across into Nevada and the great bend of the Truckee River. Charley Crocker's bold—some might say insane—stroke sent an unmistakable message that the Central Pacific was going to cross the California line and

*When the snow wouldn't let up, sheds were built to cover the uncompleted rail grade and allow work to continue.*

build in Nevada. This huge work crew, his "mobile army," worked at the Truckee River bend until spring when they returned to the Sierras and the abandoned grade, which was still buried in snow and ice.

# 6

## A MILE A DAY IN '68!

As 1867 ended, all that could be said was that it couldn't have been much worse. According to Charles Crocker, it was a year to be measured not in miles of new track but in obstacles conquered. The Central Pacific crews had laid 40-odd miles (64 km) of track, 25 miles (40 km) of which were still unconnected to the main line. The Union Pacific, on the other hand, working west through Nebraska and southern Wyoming, had put down six times as much.

The near-impossible Summit Tunnel, at least, had been finished in November. Before the year's close, however, winter's fury once again prevented the closing of a 7-mile (11.2-km) gap between the Summit Tunnel and Donner Lake. Again, the blizzards began in October and again the Chinese crew lived like moles, working, eating, and sleeping well beneath the snow's surface.

*Chinese workers watch as a train passes by in this oil painting by Joseph Becker titled* Snow Sheds on the Central Pacific Railroad in the Sierra Nevada.

At least 1868 held the promise of new terrain—
the Nevada desert. For all the heat and dryness and
desolation of the Great Basin, it was at least *not* the
Sierra Nevada mountains. How bad could it be, at
least in comparison? Charley Crocker was so opti-
mistic, he made a public announcement that his
crew would lay a mile of track each day of the year.

The Central Pacific waited impatiently for the
thaw of 1868. At the first trace of spring, they took
thousands of workers off the Nevada line and sent
them back to Cisco to, once again, attack the
uncompleted section above Donner Lake. Six thousand Chinese were driven mercilessly to remove
the thick crust of ice from the ground. Late in June,
the rails were joined. Finally, there was continuous
track from Sacramento to the Nevada state line.

While many welcomed the hot, dusty desert as
an antidote to the snowy Sierras, the Chinese found
Nevada painfully inhospitable. The tarantulas and
scorpions frightened them; the heat and dust left
their throats parched and aching.

The terrain was as desolate as the moon. And,
where there were settlements, the residents were
openly hostile to the Chinese. The Nevadans, influ-
enced by sensational newspaper accounts, looked
upon them as heathen foreigners, whose only purpose

*Indian attacks, like this one on UP workers by the Cheyenne, were not uncommon. The CP crews were alert to danger as they moved east.*

was to take their own jobs away. The white settlers rioted against the Chinese, even killing a few workers.

For all the distractions, the Chinese worked as hard as ever. Without the rugged, snowy mountains to hinder them, they made astonishing progress. On the last day of December 1868, Charley Crocker beamed as he announced the year's tally of 362 miles (579.2 km) of track—as close to a mile a day as anyone could hope for.

# 7

## A RACE TO THE FINISH

The two caught sight of each other early in 1869 as they scrambled to lay railbed just north of Ogden, Utah. The burly Irishmen of the Union Pacific grading crews looked over the rugged land to see the Central Pacific's Chinese moving methodically east. The first greeting was surely an Irishman's catcall or mocking whistle or maybe a well-tossed clump of dirt. The Chinese response was, just as surely, no response at all—at least, not at first.

In this mad dash to complete the transcontinental railroad, the Union Pacific's rough-and-tumble Irish crew had one big advantage: They understood that a race is a race and, as one player said, "The race is the thing." One side would come in first and one would finish, not second, but dead last.

The grading crews matched each other mile for mile, moving in opposite directions. Then, as so often had happened during the previous three years of railroad building, the Central Pacific was

*As the two railroad companies pushed their workers to finish on schedule, contact between the Irish and Chinese workers was often less than friendly.*

slowed by the steep, rocky terrain. As they made their stiff climb into Utah's Wasatch mountains, they worked round the clock, by the light of sagebrush fires, to keep up with the Union Pacific.

Meanwhile, in Washington, D.C., there was growing alarm over reports that in the fierce competition to lay down track, construction quality had suffered. Was it possible that the two companies, who were both deep in debt, skimped here and there? What exactly was going on?

Since the signing of the Railroad Act in 1862, three presidential administrations had tried to mediate the unceasing squabbles and controversies of the rail owners. Finally, in March 1869, a stern message came from the new president, Ulysses S. Grant: It's time to finish the transcontinental railroad, whatever it takes.

The competition was effectively ended when officials in Washington designated Promontory Point, Utah, as the meeting place for the two rail lines. From that date forward, there would be no financial incentive for speed, because the two companies would be compensated only for an agreed-upon number of miles.

News of the agreement was greeted with relief. The Central Pacific, for one, was completely worn out from their six-year effort to build through California, Nevada, and now Utah. Still, Charles Crocker was not ready to see the last month of construction become anything close to dull. He decided the time had come to make good on a bet he'd made some months before with his Union Pacific counterpart, William Durant: $10,000 says my crew can lay 10 miles (16 km) of track in one day.

It was hardly by chance that Crocker had waited to reach a flat, curveless part of Utah, where the Mormons had already prepared a smooth grade, to make his announcement. He had also waited until they were close enough to Promontory Point so that the Union Pacific would be unable to match the accomplishment.

The day was set for April 28, 1869, and Crocker and Strobridge were well prepared. All equipment was in place, and five thousand men had been pulled from other duties and brought to the worksite. If the day was successful, they'd been told, they would earn four times their daily wage.

The workers were organized with military precision: Certain men were assigned to unload rails, others to place ties, others to push handcars. There were also two eight-man rail teams (all Irish), four hundred Chinese tampers, twenty spikers. Backup teams were ready when the starters grew weary. And, of course, guests had been invited to watch what Charley Crocker felt would be a certain triumph.

The whistle blew at dawn and Charley's troops went to work. In eight minutes, the Chinese unloaded the first sixteen carsful of iron onto handcars. The pounding was so furious, bystanders said, it sounded as if bombs were going off. Handcars were then pulled by the Chinese down the track to waiting crews. These workers threw the rails, doled out bolts and spikes, or threw down fishplates with astonishing speed and precision.

Meanwhile the tie crews, who worked a few hundred yards ahead of the trackers, worked with equal exactness. Four ironmen on each side of the roadbed grasped a 600-pound (272.4-kg) rail with tongs, eased it into a spot a few inches from the previously placed rail, then went back for another. Next came the rail straighteners, followed by the levelers, who adjusted the height for smoothness. Next came the twenty spikers, each of whom drove in one spike with ten mighty blows of the maul. The fishplate men set the 22-pound (9.9-kg) joiners, which were then spiked by another crew. Last came hundreds of tampers, who were divided into three long lines. One line came down the middle, the other two on either side of the ties, smashing in the ballast with two bruising tamps before moving on. There was no room for error as each worker did precisely what was expected as quickly as humanly possible. As one army officer said, "It was just like an army marching over the ground and leaving a track built behind them . . . it was a good day's march for an army."

The bystanders, especially the representatives of the Union Pacific, were astounded as the CP crew laid rail at the pace of a walking man. By 6

A.M. they had already laid 2 miles (3.2 km) of track. Despite the hectic rush, all the workers took a full hour for lunch. When they resumed their work, rails flew as the hours ticked by.

When the whistle blew at dusk, a crowd gathered for the official measurement: 10 miles and 56 feet (17.06 km) of new track. Shouts of *Hip, hip hooray* resounded and hats were tossed into the air

*A sign marks the spot where, on April 28, 1869, CP workers laid ten miles of track.*

in celebration. During that dawn-to-dusk day, the crews had placed 25,800 ties, laid 3,520 rails, sledged 28,160 spikes, and fastened 14,080 bolts. Their record has never been matched, not even by the machines that eventually replaced the "weaponless army." To test the work's quality and to "set" the track, Crocker ordered one of his heaviest locomotives to speed along the new rails at 40 miles (64 km) an hour. The work was given high marks. Although it was really Jim Strobridge and his disciplined workforce who made this extraordinary feat possible, Crocker took the bows and gave boastful statements to the papers.

The Central Pacific rails were now just 5 miles (8 km) from Promontory Point, so work was resumed at a leisurely pace. The day of the joining had been set for May 10, not quite two weeks away. The CP's track reached Promontory first, so many of the workers took some much-deserved time off. They passed the days watching special trains carry in dignitaries for the celebrated "wedding of the rails."

# 8 PROMONTORY AND BEYOND

Governor Leland Stanford and his guests were scheduled to arrive at Promontory first, on May 8, followed by the Union Pacific chief William Durant. Mark Hopkins arrived from San Francisco, but the other two Central Pacific partners, Collis Huntington and Charles Crocker, were curiously absent. Crocker gave the excuse that he had better things to do back home in Sacramento.

In all about five hundred people attended the ceremony, including both the Irish and Chinese workers, cooks, and engineers. And, as with so much of the building of the railroad, the principle at work was that if something could go wrong, it would. The two last rails were brought up; one by the Chinese of the Central Pacific, the other by Irishmen of the Union Pacific. A photographer, who had set up his camera nearby, prepared to capture the big moment. As he made last-minute adjustments, an impatient man in the crowd shouted: "Now's the time! Take a shot!" whereupon the Chinese, who'd learned enough English to know danger when they heard it, dropped the rail and fled. Nearly half an hour passed before an interpreter could explain why they should return to the ceremony.

At last, Stanford and Durant stepped forward to tap in not one spike but four: two of California gold, one of Comstock silver, and one of mixed gold, silver, and iron from the Arizona Territory. Finally the last spike, a gold one, was set into place and readied for the final blow of the sledgehammer. Stanford, as the highest-ranking official, stepped forward to do the honor. A telegraph line had been ingeniously linked to the spike and another to the hammer so that the sound of the blow could be carried throughout the nation.

Governor Stanford raised the sledge high but then missed the spike completely. Then Durant missed it as well. Undaunted, the telegraph operator simulated the sound of a strike with his key and clicked off the word "done." An eager nation immediately began to celebrate. A magnetic ball dropped from its pole above the U.S. Capitol building, and across the land, bells tolled, cannons fired, and train whistles screeched their approval.

*Dignitaries gather in Promontory Point, Utah, on May 10, 1869, to drive in the golden spike that marked the meeting of the UP and CP rail lines.*

The workers remaining in Promontory celebrated, too, although not as lavishly as the dignitaries. By May 11, the trains carrying the railroad owners and guests all left. By nightfall, the first transcontinental train, which had started its journey in New York, made its scheduled stop in Promontory and then departed several minutes later.

The transcontinental rail line was a great success by any measure. During the rest of 1869, the railroad carried 30,000 through passengers; in 1870, it carried more than 140,000. The railroad's success meant explosive growth in California. The Big Four, who became very wealthy and powerful, each built themselves palaces on San Francisco's affluent Nob Hill. Governor Leland Stanford endowed Stanford University as a memorial to his only son, who died at an early age.

The Chinese workers weren't nearly so fortunate. Many spent the next few years working on one of the other railroad lines being built from Texas to Alaska. Then, in the early 1870s, with twenty-five thousand former railroad workers flooding the job market, unemployment in California began to rise sharply. Thousands of Chinese laborers headed for San Francisco, where, finding themselves restricted by harsh anti-Chinese exclusion laws to menial work, they crowded into Chinatown and took whatever jobs they could find.

# 9

## GHOSTS

*Men change, men die, weather changes, but a mountain is the same as permanence and time. This mountain would have taken no new shape for centuries, ten thousand centuries, the world a still, still place, time unmoving.*

In her book *China Men*, the Chinese-American author Maxine Hong Kingston tells about her grandfather, Ah Goong, who worked on the transcontinental railroad. He was not good at putting his own thoughts into words so she, one hundred years later, helps him. Through her, Ah Goong struggles to tell about "the rock," or "the ice," or the many ways there were to die high up in the Sierra mountains. The workers who had time to talk before dying, Ah Goong says, begged "Don't leave me frozen under the snow. Send my body home. . . . When you ride the fire car back to China, tell my descendants to come for me."

*Author Maxine Hong Kingston writes poignantly about the Chinese railroad workers, and especially her own grandfather, in her book* China Men.

The Central Pacific did try to make good on their promise to send workers' bodies home to China. The bones of 1,200 Chinese were reportedly shipped across the Pacific in the years following the line's completion. Many other graves, however, lay undiscovered and forgotten. All that remained were the ghosts, intent on shaking a weary traveler from complacency.

Beginning in the early 1870s, travelers reported strange sightings along the rail lines in California, Nevada, and Utah. Perhaps it was only the loneliness of the tiny, desolate station houses or the weariness of the travelers, but many began to believe the CP tracks were haunted. One man, speeding in his first-class car through the Nevada desert, thought he saw picnickers off to the side. (*Picnickers*, he thought, *here?*) As the train approached, he saw five or six straw-hatted Chinese men enjoying a large meal on beautifully decorated china.

A Utah station master recalled once that, as he and a few passengers waited on the platform, they saw a train approaching, but from the wrong direction. Before they could consider the matter, the locomotive and single car whizzed by. It was filled with merry passengers—all Chinese, playing a lively game of fantan. "It's come from the Celestial Kingdom," one bystander reported matter-of-factly.

Throughout the West, sightings and apparitions became more frequent. The Chinese, it seemed, had returned for one last look at all their heroic efforts had helped build. One tale, which appeared in Santa Fe's *Daily New Mexican* in 1880, described an eerie occurrence at Galisteo Junction. Shortly after the arrival of the evening train from Santa Fe, the station master and two friends were walking along the tracks. Suddenly they noticed in the distant western sky, over the Sierra Colorado, a large orange balloon drifting toward them. As it came closer, the stunned observers saw that the brightly colored balloon was shaped like a fish and had "fanciful characters" painted on its sides. From inside the fish-balloon's gondola, they heard loud, excited voices, all talking at once and in a language, as the newspaper wrote, "entirely unintelligible to the people on earth."

As the fish-balloon fluttered over their heads, the mysterious riders dropped two objects onto the ground below. One was a beautiful silk flower and the other a delicate blue-and-white teacup. Laughter and music from the gondola filled the evening air as the giant fish floated up and over the mountains and out of sight.

# FOR FURTHER READING

Chang, Kathleen. *The Iron Moonhunter*. San Francisco: Children's Book Press, 1977.

Hsu, Francis L.K. *The Challenge of the American Dream: The Chinese in the United States*. Belmont, Calif.: Wadsworth Publishing Co., 1971.

Kingston, Maxine Hong. *China Men*. New York: Alfred Knopf, 1980.

Meltzer, Milton. *The Chinese Americans*. New York: Crowell, 1980.

Ng, Franklin. *The Chinese American Struggle for Equality*. Vero Beach, Fla.: Rourke Corp., 1992.

Sinnott, Susan. *Extraordinary Asian Pacific Americans*. Chicago: Childrens Press, 1993.

Steiner, Stan. *Fusang: The Chinese Who Built America*. New York: Harper and Row, 1979.

Wheeler, Keith, and the editors of Time-Life. *The Old West: The Railroaders*. New York: Time-Life Books, 1973.

Wilson, John. *Chinese Americans*. Vero Beach, Fla.: Rourke Corp., 1991.

Wu, Dana Ying-Hui, and Jeffrey Dao-Seng Tung. *The Chinese-American Experience*. Brookfield, Conn.: Millbrook Press, 1993.

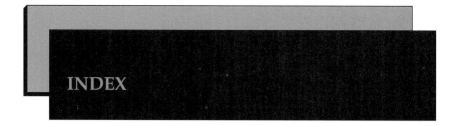

# INDEX

Ah Goong, 57

American River (California), 31

Anti-Chinese exclusion laws, 56

Blasting powder, 32, 37

California, 15, 20, 34, 39, 40, 48, 56, 59

Cape Horn, 15, 31, 32

Central Pacific Railroad (CP), 17, 19, 20, 21, 22, 23, 26, 27, 36, 39, 40, 42, 44, 46, 48, 50, 52, 53, 59

China, 25, 26, 57, 59

*China Men*, 57
    Chinatown (San Francisco), 56

Civil War, 22, 24

Crocker, Charles, 9, 13, 17, 23, 24, 25, 26, 28, 29, 34, 38, 40, 42, 44, 45, 48, 49, 52

*Daily New Mexican*, 60

Donner Lake (California), 40, 42

Donner Pass (California), 9, 11, 16, 36, 44

Durant, William, 48, 53, 54

Dutch Flat (California), 9, 32–34, 36

Dynamite, 37

Food, 28, 39, 59

Galisteo Junction (New Mexico), 60

Ghosts, 59–60

Golden spike, 60

Grant, Ulysses S., 48

Great Basin (Nevada), 44

Hopkins, Mark, 17, 53

Huntington, Collis P., 17, 39

Irish workers, 24, 25, 28, 46, 49, 53

Judah, Theodore Dehone, 16, 17, 19, 20–21, 31

Kingston, Maxine Hong, 57
Kwangtung (China), 26

Lincoln, Abraham, 19
Locomotives, 11 52, 56

Mormons, 49

Nevada, 17, 24, 41, 44, 48, 59
New York, 19, 21, 56
Nitroglycerin, 36, 37

Omaha (Nebraska), 20, 23

Pacific Railroad Act, 19–20, 48
Panama Canal, 15
Promontory Point (Utah), 48,
    49, 52, 56

Riots, 44
Rocky Mountains, 19

Sacramento (California), 17, 22,
    25, 28, 31, 34, 53
Salaries, 26, 29, 38, 39
San Francisco (California), 9,
    16, 27, 34, 35, 44, 56
Santa Fe (New Mexico), 60
Sierra Colorado, 60
Sierra Nevada, 7, 9, 13, 16, 19,
    25, 30, 35, 39, 41, 44

South America, 15, 24
Spikers, 50, 54
Stanford, Leland, 17, 22, 53, 54,
    56
Stanford University, 56
Strikes, 38–39
Strobridge, James, 7, 13, 25, 31,
    32, 36, 38, 49, 52
Summit Tunnel, 7, 9, 13, 36,
    37–38, 42
Sze Yup (China), 26–27

Telegraphs, 54
Tie crews, 49, 50–51
Transcontinental railroad, 14,
    56, 57
    completion of, 46–54
Truckee River (Nevada), 40, 41
Tunnels, 7, 9, 31–32, 35–36, 42,

Union Pacific Railroad (UP), 20,
    22, 23, 39, 42, 46, 47, 49, 50,
    53
U.S. Congress, 14, 16, 22
Utah, 46, 47, 48, 49, 59

Vanderbilt, Commodore, 21

Washington, D.C., 47, 48

Yellow Peril, 30

## ABOUT THE AUTHOR

Susan Sinnott began her publishing career as an editor for *Cricket*, a literary magazine for children. She later worked at the University of Wisconsin Press, where she managed and edited academic journals. Eventually, her own two children pulled her away from scholarly publishing and helped her rediscover the joys of reading and writing books for young people. Ms. Sinnott's books include *Extraordinary Hispanic Americans* and *Extraordinary Asian Pacific Americans*. She lives in Portsmouth, New Hampshire, with her husband and children.